Seeing the Light

New Poems for
St Michael's Church, Discoed

*Signed Jenifer and Emyr
with every regards*

Edward.

EDWARD STOREY

Published on behalf of
The Friends of St Michael's Church, Discoed
by
The Leverett Press
The Leverett
Discoed
Presteigne
LD8 2NW
UK

First published 2015

Seeing the Light

ISBN 978-0-9575375-1-4

Design and layout by Andrew Giles, The Leverett Press
for The Friends of St Michael's Church, Discoed

Printed by Orphans Press, Leominster, UK

Illustrations by Simon Dorrell

Front cover: *Discoed – detail from a sketch for a stained glass tondo*
Frontispiece: *St Michael's Church, Discoed – the Discoed Yew and church porch*
page 37: *St Michael's Church, Discoed*

Also by Edward Storey

For all the
Friends of St Michael's, Discoed

How else can we worship but in the beauty of holiness,
for what is holiness but the beauty of words, music,
silence, and the peace which comes in the presence
of the light that lightens our darkness?

Here, in this quiet place, we lift our voices in the hope
that our alleluias are acceptable, not only in shared
ceremony but in the secret of each heart
where memory and silence speak.

Contents

Welsh Hills

Like the walls of a churchyard
hills enclose a world beyond each day.

They are discreet, keeping their secrets safe
as those interred when tears said everything.

Hills not only heal but reconcile,
holding Time's laughter and a loving shared.

What ever journeys of the heart we take
they will be always there to prove there is

a light that will outlive the dark.

Seeing the Light

The artist does not seek, he finds.   Picassso

It is the same with prayer
(as I have said before),
sometimes we try too hard
by asking more than listening.

Rather than close our eyes
it helps to open them and find
the answer in another place
which always takes us by surprise.

And suddenly, like drawing back
the curtains after sleep,
we see a flood of light, as bright
as sun-drenched rain on morning grass.

The Concert

What can these stones hold
that is more harmonious than silence?

Outside, the wind is tearing apart
the winter sky. But here

the music of Byrd and Tallis
tames the violence of the universe.

Sounds of virginals and lute
in candlelight, calm all our fears,

help, we believe, to comfort those
who sit alone in this rapt audience –

and, being elsewhere,
are no longer one.

Seeing Music

How often you've been here but not here
when music becomes visible
and there's a presence in the empty space
between the sound of one note and the one to come.

I now know what Rilke meant –
It's a *breathing of statues, perhaps . . .*
Or *stillness in pictures . . .* Someone always
comes to life when song becomes more than song.

But how difficult it is for one
to applaud for two. We'd prefer the silence
to remain intimate, for the last note
to delay meeting the note unsung,

for the statue to keep breathing.

The Window

(for Simon Dorrell)

Once in a blue moon a miracle happens.
Stone mellows into glass through which light flows
and all is changed before our marvelled eyes.

A village sleeps beneath a veil of stars
and it's no fantasy the scene reveals
moonlight on sheep that graze in lunar grass.

Here night and day are magically conjoined,
not just within the compass of earth's tide
but in the sacred union of bread and wine.

See how a shaft of sunlight fills the air
with memories we thought would never wake.
Stones hide their secrets from us only when

we let their silence keep us in the dark.
Between each end of day this new eye shows
all that once was, and will be, are made one.

A Churchyard Resurrection

The first snowdrops have arrived
like a group of weary pilgrims
who have walked all winter
on their way to Walsingham.

They stand with their heads bowed
waiting to receive a blessing from the sun,
for Spring's doors to suddenly open
at first light's resurrection.

They have returned to this hill
because their faith has not faltered
nor earth failed in its promises.

We, too, know the dark days are over,
can begin our own pilgrimage
away from the heart's hunger.

At the Table

When this table was part of a green oak
two hundred years ago, its boughs
were warmed by quieter days than those
that have outlived its leaves. Yet,
through its metamorphosis, we feel
new life is breathed into its soul.

Out of the knots and muscles of a tree
we've made a meeting-place where minds
can be as honest as the live-long day.
All tables listen with a knowing eye
for they have secrets they must keep
until the falling of the last oak tree.

Christ chose a table for a gathering
of his disciples, to explain
their sharing of the bread and wine,
and why a tree would bear one fruit
which then must die that other guests
might also gather there and dine.

Nocturne for Maundy Thursday

The hill is quiet tonight.
A fox appears from badgers' copse
and zig-zags down a field
which earlier was full of sheep.
He sniffs the air, aware
that something's not quite right.

Too late. He can't escape
the headlights waiting in the dark
nor the single gun-shot
that makes the hillside emptier still.

It is disturbing now to think
tomorrow we'll commemorate
another death upon a different hill.

Mary's Lament

You ask me why I weep.
I weep because my son is dead –
the child I bore with sorrow in my heart
when stars were full of premonitions
and wise men kept their counsel.

The heart can be a wilderness
when love dies, a lonely place
where comfort cannot soothe or tears console.
These are the days of desolation
no gift of language can dispel.

I weep because a mother must
when numbed by grief. Who has not lost
can never feel the pain of loss,
the emptiness that always hurts
when nothing's left of all that was.

So how shall I find peace?
How live or be? And silence says:
Arise! Take, eat, and go your way.
Love does not die for where your tears now fall
a whiter rose will grow.

Poppies on Calvary

Were there poppies on Calvary?
If they first grew in Ancient Greece
because the blood of young Adonis stained the soil,
surely Golgotha must have felt the seeds
of that bright flower stir when Christ's blood woke
earth's sorrow from its sleep.

Were there poppies on Calvary?
If they have grown in Flanders' fields
since earth received the lives of those who died
that all those still unborn might live,
surely red petals must have bled upon that hill
where Christ was sacrificed.

Were there poppies on Calvary?
If, where his tears flowed down
and his blood blossomed into wine,
surely we share that love which came –
first with a wreath of thorns,
and then a crown.

Missing a Hill

Not much happens here.
A shepherd comes back with his dog;
it's one of the small events of the day
that will be missed when the day comes
and he no longer steps into the hour
to remind us how all time
is made up of moments like this.

He is as constant as the sun
and, though he moves slower with the years,
were he not to appear
it would be like missing a hill
that had always been there –
a man whose presence says all
we still need to hear.

When Light Returns

Yes, there were shadows.
What valley has not known dark hours
when light failed to heal
and sorrow made time stumble?

Yet shadows do not last.
Hills only sleep when day
is somewhere else.
Light does not compromise.

Looking back from this hill,
Fields, houses and farms,
take their place in a world
that is always changing.

All will arrive or leave in their time
yet light will survive, not from the sun
and litany of colours in stained-glass
but from an eye that never knows the dark.

Easter Sunday Morning

Daybreak. The headstones are so still
they could be listening, waiting to see
which might be first to wake or roll away
to show an empty sepulchre.

A woman arrives and opens the church door.
What will she find? Flowers on a window-sill
and hints of coloured light upon the floor?
Or will she stand, like Mary Magdalene – afraid
and, for a moment, be unsure?

Such early sunlight can deceive the eye.
there's more than emptiness for those
who have not been to Calvary before.

Evening Service in the Churchyard

(for Stephen and Dilys)

Under the great tree, a Victorian headstone
gathers the low rays of the sun
and the shadow of someone standing near
now falls upon it like a silhouette
hung on the walls of a velvet drawing-room.

For one unnerving moment it appears
as if the stone has welcomed its next guest
or, in this eldritch light, maybe
the present tenant has outwitted death
and stepped outside for one last bonus breath.

No more than a coincidence perhaps
but somehow a reminder to us all
that nothing lasts beyond our fingertips.
Sharing this evening service out of doors
we are aware that only love survives.

Towards Nightfall

A shallow tide of light flows through the grass
as earth becomes a sea-bed for the night.

Now shadows weave a net between the trees
to catch our dreams and sell them to the moon.

How many lives did we dream-up today?
too many for the night to make come true.

Time is too practical, for we all know
that what is wished for clocks will soon destroy.

But there is love beyond the hands that touch.
Each tide will turn, receding inch by inch

until the moon gives up our fantasies
and wet grass ripples in the waking sun.

Who then will fathom what the night explored
while in our sleep we swam among the stars?

There are no explanations we should trust
when night is always deeper than we thought.

Another Way of Singing

Why am I trying to make songs out of stones
when the full foliage of summer sings more easily?
Two blackbirds tease me from a nearby tree,
swallows turn phrases in air as fluently
as any gifted tongue, and the sky
needs no coloured images to illustrate
the legends of a dying sun.

More than blackbirds contribute to my random hymn
Robin and wren add their own harmonies,
as does a bee. If flowers had voices they, too,
would blend their fragrance into cadences.
Only a priestly magpie, always out of tune,
struts on the lawn as if ordained to be
master of this ceremony.

It is the turn of stones to listen now –
walls, tower, spire, porch and roof
locked in their hours of silences.
Where would they be if summer's branches
did not enhance their bare antiquity?
I, in my listening, willingly admit
without what's given me there'd be no song.

Bringing Home a Nightingale's Eggshell

(for Ann)

You cradled in the nest of your hands
nearly the whole of a small shell
that had released its song to the sky.

Thin as an onion skin, it held
the soft white membrane of birth
still mother-bird-warm and frail.

Too delicate for us to comprehend
how a song-bird grew from a brown pearl
to free itself on Hergest Hill.

And what of the song?   Was it as fragile
as the shell your hands brought home?
The sky is such a hollow place to fill

some songs seem destined to die young.
Wings fail to reach where they would wish to fly
and all horizons tease the keenest eye.

Yet while this shell, now like a tiny skull,
sits on my shelf, its joy can never be
silenced by predator or grief.

Like the Hare and Skylark

A hare, tense as the fuse
to a stick of dynamite,
is crouched in a furrow. She knows
the risk of moving too soon.
One twitch of muscle, one breath
too visible, would instantly transmit her fear
to whoever sought to flush her out.

Above her, a skylark
taut as a string about to snap,
gauges how long it can sustain
its song on trembling air.
Which is the safer bet – the earth or sky?
Again there is nowhere to hide
for one so talented.

All who trespass near the sun
learn to be wary of the heat.
Between the hare and lark
exists a mutual fear –
both are as vulnerable as all
who wish to prove they are alive.
It is a risk we take who need to fly.

Accepting What We Are

(for Angela)

At the end of summer what have we left
but a collection of summers
which we compare with all the ones we've known –

the wettest years with those of desert drought,
or holidays abroad with ones at home
(which often gained by being on our own).

Even the photographs were seldom true.
Mysterious shadows crept into the frame
spoiling what would have been a perfect view.

Then we may think of those adventurous years
when we were young enough to take
our annual holidays in Alpine snow,

smiling at how easily we climbed
those white peaks propping up the sky.
Who would believe that of us now?

But it's unwise to brood on such regrets
when what we are is what we always were –
and what we were has made us what we are.

So all we need to settle in our minds
is are we halfway up, or down, a hill
and make the most of summers left to share.

The Only Landscape We Can Trust

(for Kirsty Williams)

The language I knew has receded
and I am a stranger to the memories
that disappeared with the landscape
into thin air, into a bigger sky
than I could understand. Words,
once gleaned from the fields
and taken home to a warm house,
have faded, like flowers pressed in a book
for our own preservation.

The day came when ploughed furrows
could not accept the seeds being planted,
when songs taught by a fireside
belonged to another country.
Why do worlds change more than ourselves?
We look with the same expectations
at a different horizon and know
new words must be fashioned to unearth
thoughts buried for a season in the dark.

And the language I speak now would not
be understood by those who shared
those half-forgotten boundaries.
Rooms where the songs were first sung
have gone like voices once taken for granted.
We learn the only landscape we can trust
is the one we take with us in the heart,
where neither wind nor winter will erode
words that were with us from the start.

Where the Blue Cedar Grew

Now it is gone we can see
how shadows take up space as well as light.

It was more than the tree's presence
in a garden where it didn't belong.

Its heavy branches hid the sun
and halved the daylight on the lawn.

Sad such a fine tree had to die
before its time but we agree

it never looked at home, its dark roots
pining to be somewhere else.

Knowing how some spaces
need to be filled to ease their emptiness

we sit where evening light
casts shadows of a different kind

and are reminded now
of warmer presences we miss.

A Man Who Loved Things

(for Jane Thorpe, in memory of Adrian)

He was a man who loved wood.
Not wood gnarled and generous with splinters
but wood that smelt of the seasons
and the fruit of walnut, apple or oak;
wood that was willing to be shaped
by lathe or chisel, plane or blade
into a bowl or sheltered garden-seat,
or something more elaborate –
the mediaeval rood in a country church.
Wood, that in dying, had another life
and so outlived the muscle of its making.

He was a man who loved clay.
Not clay that burdened his walking-boots
but clay that smelt of the earth
where roots had clung for sustenance;
clay that was waiting to be shaped
into a work of art by craftsmen's hand
that would in quietness turn a perfect vase
which, in its metamorphosis, we can't forget.
It was through such labour he enjoyed
the common artefact made beautiful,
bringing new life to everything he touched.

He was a man who loved talk.
Not the tittle-tattle of words that evaporate
because they have no substance
but the talk of wonder in a world
where rivers, meadows, woodlands, farms,
made him believe in a paradise
needing no mythical disguise
for the heart to understand
it is earth's silences that make us wise.
Nature for him had made it plain to see
How, through our love of things, we do not die.

Shorelines

Part of us is always awakened
when we stand at the sea's edge.

Some somnambulant cell stirs,
as if being told it is going home.

The tide turns. Waves beckon
and we begin to feel as if

all the waiting was worthwhile,
that the end is without question.

But, being unsure, we take one step
back from the foam,

for land is what we trust most –
rocks that have withstood fire.

Ebb-tide

(for Gill Tennant-Eyles)

It is all that was left as the sea slipped
into the darkness beyond earth's shore –
Time's footprint now a crooked claw
trapped on the edge of night
and crystalized by more than frost
or one star slowly burning out.

So many million tides have turned
and taken with them on their flow
the silent histories of all who stood
feeling the lure of the moon, the pull
of promises that seldom do come true,
though far-off days are calling still.

Although these ripples now lie hard as stone
they do not stop the rhythm of the waves
which never fail to roll back memories
we thought had been erased by morning light.
Here on this furrowed beach we learn to share
those presences no tide can drown.

(based on a ceramic sculpture by Gill Tennant-Eyles)

Two's Company, One's a Crowd

(in memory of my sister)

The power of solitude is lost
if we're aware of absences.
Time then becomes loneliness
and it is wiser to share silence
with one who understands the need
sometimes to feel alone.

Solitude should be absolute.
Resting a moment on these rocks
above an iridescent sea,
I cannot free my mind of one
who will not leave my thoughts
and still is part of me.

I'd gladly grant her half
of what this day has given.
But more than distance makes the gift
impossible. There are some halves
Time never can make whole
or bonds of love now heal.

All Those Lifetimes

If a shell, or pebble from a seashore
is all that is left of a summer,
   it is better than nothing.

If an image of a landscape
is all that is left of a country,
   it is better than nothing.

If a letter, or flower pressed in a book
is all that is left of a lover,
   it is better than nothing.

If a photograph now out of fashion
is all that is left of perfection,
   it is better than nothing.

And if all those keepsakes are lifetimes
of what might have happened,
   they are still better than nothing.

The Sculptor

(for Antonia Salmon)

The world moves in the stillness you have made.
    As clouds unfold or form without a sound
    so your hands shape earth's clay into a life
that holds more than our minds can comprehend.

For what is stillness if it is not found
    within each burnished moment you create?
    Silence has nowhere to exist until
those moments of your art and vision meet.

Hands touch more tenderly when minds can see
    how close hands are when words do not confuse
    our feelings silence nurtured in the heart.
From your perception a new stillness grows.

Distance may separate as much as age
    but in the quiet perfection of your gift
    there is a marriage nothing can surpass.
Chance has no other explanation left.

The Composer

(for Barry Ferguson on his 70th birthday)

There will always be light in those arches of stone
and a voice shining where no lamp could survive
the centuries until music was made luminous –
a light heard rather than seen, which gave joy
to all who had prayed, married or mourned
where ceremony was always prominent,
for none more than that sad queen now lying
in an English cathedral, under the arms of Spain.

Some lights have echoes far beyond those shadows
which beckon when hearts need to be comforted.
Today I send you this poem of bright seeds
gathered at leisure from Time's crevices.
Few ghosts now chill the air and we can return
to where the music made one night lives on,
where, under that thrice-blessed tower of stone,
Kate becomes Katharine again.

Barry Ferguson's "Katharine of Aragon" Cantata was
first performed in Peterborough Cathedral on 6th July 1972,
with Katharine (Kate) Bown as Queen Katharine.
I was privileged to be invited to write the libretto.

One Act of Love is Light Enough

(in memory of my brother John)

Would not a wise man accept three lanterns to lighten his path
on a dark night, rather than one? Li-Shu-K'ung*

I still remember how you offered me
three lanterns to lighten my path on a dark night.

You, a philosopher, who thought I would be
wise enough to take advantage of such light.

Yet how could I be sure your lamps would not
blow out on that last journey I must make?

I chose instead eight angels in stained-glass
who took their brightness from the sun.

They, too, sometimes could not sustain my faith
and slowly turned to shadows, then to stone.

Each destination soon became a kind of death
from which escape was more than a coincidence.

And am I wiser to believe arriving's only half
of all we know? I now recall a dying man who said:

'What does it come to in the end?
one gentle act of love is light enough.

Just hold my hand and talk me through the dark.'

(*Li-Shu-K'ung was one of the pseudonyms used by
my brother who was a philosopher and theologian.*)

A Centenary of Leaves – 1914-2014

They have been falling, falling
since one false move turned all the weathers round
and summer never could be so again.

Child, fruit or songbird falling
are all of one season in the spinning fortune
of earth and love on Time's frail axle.

Of all fresh leaves that first unfurled
on Spring's green boughs a century ago,
I think of those who, on their shining branches,

made summer sing and saw our days
prolong the hours beyond our Eden tree
before blood festered in the vein.

Then lovers knew their hiding in tall grass
protected them from all eyes but the moon's –
that most discreet of Peeping Toms.

Yet when leaves fall we ask once more
if choices we first made were always wise
when many of those moments were too shy.

Of all the leaves that fall, whether as loves,
griefs, promises or truths, we know their kind
will never unfold again to be

desired fruits upon tomorrow's tree.
Stones take the place of tears when summers fail
to hide the words we never learnt to say.

You Must Take My Word for It

'When I go hence, let this be my parting word,
that what I have seen is unsurpassable.'

Rabindranath Tagore

How difficult to describe the unsurpassable
when language pales in an evening light
flooding the grass in a golden tide
beneath whose waves a million stars
     remain invisible.

How much better to accept what is impossible
through eyes, ears, images or words,
and let the heart contain its gratitude
in silence. There are no adjectives
     for what's intangible.

How frustrating now to think no excusable
rhyme or metaphor can record
those moments when the mind longs to express
the joy of days we may not see again
     and, in their passing lose.

Envoi

Let me praise the light that will still be here
    when I no longer see the light
spreading like honey on the grass.

Let me praise the stars that will still be bright
    when I no longer share the night
with those who sleep within each house.

Let me praise the years that I've been given
    to sing of stillness and the flight
of days that have been bountiful

in bringing blessings to this holy hill,
    that others yet to come will know
we shared in this perpetual miracle.